# Meandering on the Ex

CU00798642

## Chapters

**(1) Dawlish to Dawlish Warren**

**(2) Dawlish Warren to Cockwood and Starcross**

**(3) Starcross to Powderham**

**(4) Powderham to Turf**

**(5) Turf to Exminster and the Bird reserve**

**(6) Exminster to Exeter Ship Canal Swing Bridge**

**(7) Exeter Ship Canal Swing Bridge to Topsham**

**(8) Topsham to Exton**

**(9) Exton to Lympstone**

**(10) Lympstone to Exmouth.**

## DISCLAIMER

The contents of the book are correct at time of publication. However we cannot be held responsible for any errors or omissions or changes in details or for any consequences of any reliance on the information provided. We have tried to be accurate in the book, but things can change and would be grateful if readers advise me of any inaccuracies they may encounter.

I have taken every care to ensure the walks are safe and achievable by walkers with a reasonable level of fitness. But with outdoor activities there is always a degree of risk involved and the publisher accepts no responsibility for any injury caused to readers while following these walks.

## SAFETY FIRST

All the walks have been covered to ensure minimum risk to walkers that follow the routes.

Always be particularly careful if crossing main roads, but remember traffic can also be dangerous even on minor country lanes.

If in the country and around farms be careful of farm machinery and livestock (take care to put dog on lead) and observe the **Country Code**.

Also ensure you wear suitable clothing and footwear, I would advise wearing walking boots which protect from wet feet and add extra ankle support over uneven terrain.

There are a few rules that should be observed if walking alone advise somebody were you are walking and approximate time you will return. Allow plenty of time for the walk especially if it is further and or more difficult than you have walked before. Whatever the distance make sure you have enough daylight hours to complete the walk safely. When walking along a country road always walk on the right to face oncoming traffic, the only exception is on a blind bend were you cross to the left to have a clear view and can be seen from both directions.

If bad weather should come in making visibility difficult, do not panic just try to remember any features along route and get out the map to pinpoint the area but be sure before you move off, that you are moving in the right direction.

Unfortunately accidents can still happen even on the easiest of walks, if this is the case make sure the person in trouble is safe before seeking help. If carrying a mobile phone dial 999 or 112 European Union emergency number will connect you to any network to get you help.

Unmapped walks we recommend that you take the relevant Ordnance Survey map and compass with you, even if you have a Smartphone, digi-walker or G.P.S all of which can fail on route.

# Introduction

This book covers the 20 mile walk from start to finish on what I call the Horseshoe of Delights named because of its shape around the Exe Estuary Trail. Take a walk or go by bike the variation is so different to any other walking trail. Go by bus or train and walk just a short section of the Exe Estuary Trail, take the ferry and make a circular walk out on a day's outing for the whole family. So start at home and customize your planned walk or cycle ride by making it circular with the aid of the bus, train or ferry. Go out for the day and maybe walk from Dawlish to Exminster, then catch the foot ferry over to Topsham across the River Exe before crossing back and catching the bus back to Dawlish or Newton Abbot.

If you would like a different route then catch a bus to Exeter and walk to Topsham then on out to Darts Farm Complex, walk around the Bowling Green Marshes via the Goats Walk then back to Exeter or on to Darts Farm to catch a bus back into Exeter. All of this can be put together to create your own routes using the transport of your choose and depending on what you want to see and do along the way.

Maybe if you are still undecided then take a circular route from Exminster go across on the foot ferry to Topsham and then walk back to Exeter via the Exeter Ship Canal Swing Bridge back to Exminster. If you would like to extend the walk cross the road at the swing bridge and follow the canal path into the Exeter Quay or maybe on into the city, and then catch the bus back home or the start of your walk.

If you are a walker and a bird lover then take time to explore the Exminster and Powderham Marshes and/or Bowling Green Marsh, all of which have a great collection of birds with different species throughout the seasons. To get the full details of these marshes then pick-up a leaflet Exe Estuary Nature Reserve Trail Guide available from many information centres. Please remember The Exe Estuary is recognised as being of international importance for wildlife and as such is designated as a special protection area. Enjoy your time on the Exe Estuary but please be aware of your impact on this fragile environment.

Take your litter home
Do not disturb the birds or wildlife
Stay on the paths and only use the designated area for your activity
Be aware of bylaws such as species restrictions when fishing.

Be safe and take care to you and all users on the trail.

Happy Walking.

# Meandering on the Exe Estuary Trail

## Chapter 1 Dawlish to Dawlish Warren

**Park & Start Grid ref; SX 966774**

**Distance: 1.5 Miles**

**Level: Easy**

**Time: 1 hour 30 minutes**

**Terrain: Urban roads, cycle track and through wooded area paths.**

**Maps. O.S Explorer 110 Torquay and Dawlish.**

**Refreshments: Plenty of cafes, pubs and restaurants in Dawlish Warren.**

Dawlish cycle trail out over the Estuary.

### Dawlish Warren

### Access to start

Exit the M5 motorway at junction 30 at Sandygate and take the A379 signposted Dawlish. Follow A379 to meet A3015 onto Rydon Lane before re-joining the A379 again at Bridge Road, then stay on A379 through Exminster, Kenton and Starcross on into Dawlish to turn right up Sandy Lane to car park just before leisure centre.

### Nearby places

### Dawlish

This was a town in the 18th century that was just a small fishing port which then later grew into a well-known seaside resort. The name Dawlish is derived from the Welsh river name meaning black stream, this is now called Dawlish Water or it is locally known as The Brook.

## Teignmouth

Teignmouth is situated on the north bank of the estuary mouth of the River Teign. The town like Dawlish started out as a fishing port associated with the Newfoundland Cod Industry, but it then went on to be a fashionable resort of some note in the Georgian times. Teignmouth was also the first town in Devon to receive the Fairtrade Town status.

Teignmouth still as its own Grand Pier with amusements and children's rides, positioned in the centre of the beach. The Grand Pier was built in 1865 to 1867, it did suffer badly in the storms early in 2014 but is now restored and open again.

**Part of the National Cycle Route 2 linking the Southwest Coast Path out of Dawlish.**

**The Walk**

**(1)**

The walk starts not on the Exe Estuary Trail but in Dawlish, this path then is part of the Southwest Coast Path. Park in the car park off Sandy Lane opposite Dawlish Town Football ground and Leisure Centre. Exit car park and turn right for about 60 metres to reach the road junction on to the main Exeter to Dawlish road, at junction turn left and continue to follow the pavement on up to Henty Avenue. Cross the Avenue and then after just 20 metres cross the main road at the pedestrian crossing. Once across the road turn right and then head for the narrow path between the Rockstone Flats on the left and a large white house on the right. Continue to follow the upper path ignoring the footpath that drops down over the bridge to the sea.

**(2)**

Stay on the upper path as it slowly rises up a slope and then a few steps going past a few bungalows on the left with very good views out over the sea on the right. Follow the path to the end to reach the National Cycle route 2 and then turn right, stay on the track now for about a mile on past the Langstone Cliff Hotel on the left before reaching the start or end of the large car park at Dawlish Warren. Continue to follow path between car park and holiday chalets on the left to reach a roundabout in Dawlish Warren.

**(3)**

Turn left at the roundabout and crossing the road to the pavement, walk just a few metres to reach the Dawlish Warren Road the main road through the holiday complex. Then just follow the pavement on the right on past the holiday camps for nearly half a mile to reach the Dawlish Sands camp the last on the right. At this point cross the road carefully to pick-up the well signposted Exe Estuary Trail on the other side of the road.

**Picking up the Exe Estuary Trail out of Dawlish Warren.**

# Meandering on the Exe Estuary Trail

## Chapter 2 Dawlish Warren to Cockwood, Starcross

**Park & Start Grid ref; SX 978793**

**Distance: 2 Miles**

**Level: Easy**

**Time: 1 hour 45 minutes**

**Terrain: Urban roads, cycle track and through quaint little villages.**

**Maps.  O.S Explorer 110 Torquay and Dawlish.**

**Refreshments: Plenty of cafes, pubs and restaurants in Dawlish Warren Cockwood and Starcross.**

Cockwood Harbour.

**Starcross looking out towards Exmouth.**

### Access to start

Leave M5 motorway at junction 30 and take the 1st exit on roundabout onto Sidmouth Road, and then at the next roundabout take the 4th exit onto the A379. Then take the slip road to the A3015 Rydon Lane. At the next roundabout take the 2nd exit onto A379 Bridge Road. Then pass through two roundabouts but stay on the A379, after about 7 miles turn left onto Church Road at Cockwood and follow Dawlish Warren Road on into Dawlish Warren.

### Places Nearby

### Dawlish Warren Nature Reserve

The Dawlish Warren Nature Reserve is in the heart of the complex, with grassland, sand dunes, mudflats which is centred over 1.5 miles of sandy beach across the mouth of the Exe Estuary. There are wildfowl and wading birds, and the birds come in there thousands to feed or on migration or just to spend the winter here. Then there is the sand dunes with hundreds of types of flowering plants. The Nature Reserve has a lot of different habitats which include salt marsh, fresh water ponds, wet meadows and woodland. There is no access to the golf course and mudflats and dogs must be kept on leads over must of the Nature Reserve. The Visitors Centre is very helpful and stocks a number of leaflets and other publications.

**The Walk**

**(1)**

Once you are at the end of Dawlish Warren, on the right is Dawlish Sands Holiday Camp, right opposite to the entrance is the Exe Estuary Trail signposted with the start going through the gate. The Exe Estuary Trail then runs in parallel with the Dawlish Warren Road hidden behind a hedge which looks out over the fields on the left and up to Easdon House. Continue to follow the pathway for about 600 metres to reach a gate which exits out onto the road. Take extreme care and cross the road to re-join the Exe Estuary Trail on the other side of the road which after about a half a mile emerges from the enclosed trail out onto a pavement next to the road. Stay on the pavement to the end, and then continue along the road to enter the quaint little village of Cockwood, with its charming buildings and pubs all in the area around the harbour.

**(2)**

Stay on the narrow road around the harbour, but beware of traffic as you continue along Church Road to reach the road junction onto Exeter Road. Turn right at the road junction and after about 150 metres turn left by crossing the pedestrian crossing. Then continue to follow the path for about half a mile all the way into Starcross.

**The view across the Exe Estuary from Starcross.**

# Chapter 3 Starcross to Powderham

**Park & Start Grid ref; SX 976819**

**Distance: 1.5 Miles**

**Level: Easy**

**Time: 1 hour**

**Terrain: Country roads, cycle track and through quaint little village.**

**Maps.  O.S Explorer 110 Torquay and Dawlish.**

**Refreshments: Plenty of cafes, pubs and restaurants in Starcross and Powderham.**

Powderham Castle.

**Powderham Church.**

**Access to start**

Leave M5 motorway at junction 30 and take the 1st exit on roundabout onto Sidmouth Road, and then at the next roundabout take the 4th exit onto the A379. Then take the slip road to the A3015 Rydon Lane. At the next roundabout take the 2nd exit onto A379 Bridge Road. Then pass through two roundabouts but stay on the A379, after about 6 miles you drive into Starcross with the car park on left just before the railway station.

## Places Nearby

### Option 1

This is a slight diversion away from the Exe Estuary Trail, leave Starcross via gate out of car park and follow trail to reach Powderham gatehouse on left and take the driveway past house, please remember this is a permissive path that takes you on up to the farm shop and café and then leads on to Powderham Castle. Return back the same way to re-join the Exe Estuary Trail.

### Starcross

This is a little village on the edge of the Exe Estuary with the A379 road and the London to Penzance railway running through the centre. There is Starcross Railway Station and also Starcross to Exmouth Ferry pedestrian only this operates from near the rail station over the bridge.

One of the most outstanding features in Starcross is the **Italianate** pumping house, this is the best surviving building from Brunel's unsuccessful Atmospheric Railway. All this is now commemorated in the Atmospheric Railway Inn opposite the railway station and not in the pump house which is now used for the Starcross Fishing and Cruising Clubs.

**The Walk**

**(1)**

Leave Starcross go past the railway station and ferry terminal, then on past the public toilets on the right to continue carefully through the Atmospheric Railway Inn car park on the left keeping to the green marked pathway to stay up high past the public car park to finally reach a gate at the end of the footpath. Go through the gate and carefully cross road turning right and then walk along path for about 500 metres, then just before a Gate house on left there is an **option 1** to turn left to follow the permissive driveway on up to Powderham Castle with the farm shops and café. But to continue with the walk then just stay on the road and follow for about a mile into Powderham with the church off to the left, and the Exe Estuary Trail signposted off to the right which is just past a small parking layby.

**Tower still in Powderham Park.**

# Chapter 4 Powderham to the Turf

**Park & Start Grid ref; SX 963860**

**Distance: 1.2 Miles**

**Level: Easy**

**Time: 1 hour**

**Terrain: Country roads, cycle track and pathway along the wall.**

**Maps. O.S Explorer 110 Torquay and Dawlish.**

**Refreshments: Turf now only open certain times of the year.**

**The new bridge over the railway lines on the Exe Estuary Trail.**

## The Turf

## Access to start

Leave The M5 motorway at junction 30 take 1st exit on roundabout onto Sidmouth Road, then at next roundabout take 4th exit onto the A379. Go off at slip road to A3015 Rydon Lane, then at roundabout take 2nd exit onto A379 Bridge Road. Then has you enter Exminster and go under the M5 motorway at roundabout exit 1st junction to Swans Nest, go past pub over bridge and follow country lane to car park. The only way then to The Turf is to walk or cycle.

## Places Nearby

The Exeter Ship Canal was the first canal to be built in Britain since Roman times, the first section dating back to 1566. It enabled vessels to navigate to the wharfs at Exeter Quay for the River Exe was obstructed by shoals and fishing weirs, purposely enlarged by the Countess of Devon, Isabella De Fortibus, so trade would be diverted to the Port of Topsham from which she derived an income!

In 1827 the extension was opened along with The Turf Hotel providing accommodation for the Lock Keeper, and the crews of the many sailing vessels that were to enter the Canal.

## The Turf

The food and drink is locally sourced whenever available. All the real ales are from Devon or Cornwall, there is also 2 local wines as well as locally produced cider and apple juice.

Nearly all the food is homemade and supplied locally. When the weather is fine there are the very popular outside BBQ. Food is served every lunchtime and evening but not on Sunday evenings.

The Turf closes from the 1st December until mid-February.

**The Walk**

**(1)**

Once on the Exe Estuary Trail out of Powderham we then cross the new bridge over what was a dangerous railway level crossing. The trail then splits with the cycle track down low and following a very nice tarmac levelled surface, with the other path for pedestrians following the old wall along the Exe Estuary with views back to Starcross and on to towards The Turf. This then is a very easy walk taking in the views and the wildlife, quietly soaking up the fresh air for about 1 mile before reaching The Turf for light refreshments.

**View from Turf Lock up the Exeter Ship Canal towards Exeter.**

# Chapter 5 the Turf to Exminster

**Park & Start Grid ref; SX 962879**

**Distance: 1.5 Miles**

**Level: Easy**

**Time: 1 hour 15 minutes**

**Terrain: cycle track and pathway along the canal tow-path.**

**Maps.  O.S Explorer 110 Torquay and Dawlish.**

**Refreshments: Swans Nest Exminster.**

The Topsham ferry terminal near Exminster.

**The River Exe and the Exeter Ship Canal separated by the Lock Keepers Cottage.**

## Access to start

Leave The M5 motorway at junction 30 take 1st exit on roundabout onto Sidmouth Road, then at next roundabout take 4th exit onto the A379. Go off at slip road to A3015 Rydon Lane, then at roundabout take 2nd exit onto A379 Bridge Road. Then has you enter Exminster and go under the M5 motorway at roundabout exit 1st junction to Swans Nest, go past pub over bridge and follow country lane to car park. The only way then to The Turf is to walk or cycle.

## Places Nearby

### Exminster

This is an ancient village associated with a Saxon minster or religious community founded back in the 8<sup>th</sup> century. In the 14<sup>th</sup> century it became the seat of the Courtenay family. Overlooking the Exe Estuary on the northwest side of the village is the former Devon County Asylum opened in 1845, which now today forms part of a housing complex.

### Exminster Nature Reserve

'The Exminster and Powderham Marshes were once part of the Exe estuary, but have been reclaimed and improved and now form part of the Exe Estuary nature reserve [sic]; they include grazing marshes with freshwater ditches, and some small areas of arable land on the higher ground to the west.

'The wetland bird spectacle is at its best in winter, when hundreds of ducks and flocks of lapwings, curlews and black-tailed godwits can be seen on the marshes. In spring, the marshes are particularly important for regionally scarce nesting lapwings and redshanks

**Exminster Nature Reserve and Marshes.**

**The Walk**

**(1)**

Leaving The Turf with its good refreshments and beautiful sunshine proved to be difficult. But the walk continued on along the Exeter Ship Canal tow-path taking the views across the wetlands off to the left, and then the magnificent River Exe over to our right. This is just a very straight forward walk of about 1.5 miles along the Exeter Ship Canal until you reach the small car park on the left. The car park leads off to the road to access to Exminster Marshes Nature Reserve, or continue on to the Swans Nest Public House, then if you continue this road you come into the outskirts of Exminster.

**(2)**

To continue the walk do not exit at car park but stay on the Exeter Ship Canal tow-path and walk for about another 500 metres to reach the Topsham Ferry Terminal on the right, this is just before the Lock Keeper's Cottage, this is positioned between the River Exe and the Exeter Ship Canal.

**Exeter Ship Canal looking back in the direct of The Turf.**

# Chapter 6 Exminster to Exeter Ship Canal Swing Bridge

**Park & Start Grid ref; SX 940894**

**Distance: 1.8 Miles**

**Level: Easy**

**Time: 1 hour 30 minutes**

**Terrain: cycle track and pathway along the canal tow-path.**

**Maps.  O.S Explorer 110 Torquay and Dawlish.**

**Refreshments: Swans Nest Exminster.**

Exeter Ship Canal Swing Bridge.

**Exeter Ship Canal and River Exe side by side.**

**Access to start**

Leave The M5 motorway at junction 30 take 1st exit on roundabout onto Sidmouth Road, then at next roundabout take 4th exit onto the A379. Go off at slip road to A3015 Rydon Lane, then at roundabout take 2nd exit onto A379 Bridge Road. Then just before the Exeter Canal Swing Bridge turn left signpost Water Works near a snack wagon and park around the corner near the canal.

**Places Nearby**

**Option 2**

Exit the gate at Exeter Ship Canal Swing Bridge and cross over the pedestrian crossing to follow the canal into the Exeter Quay. The return route is via the River Exe and then on the canal tow-path back to the pedestrian crossing the total walk is about 4 miles, but there is the option to extend on into Exeter City to see the Exeter Cathedral, Parliament Street, what was once Mol's Coffee shop and the Turks Head and many more places to see. This is the City full of history and modern life, so why not stay over to get the full value of the city.

**The Walk**

**(1)**

This section of the walk continues on from Topsham Ferry Terminal near Exminster and follows the Exeter Ship Canal tow-path. This is a really beautiful section with the canal twisting and turning following the shape of the River Exe. Both the Exeter Ship Canal and the River Exe run in parallel with each other for most of the walk along this section. Then as you walk on further you go under the M5 motorway which after all these years is starting to blend in with the background. Then it's on to the next wide bend in the canal where there are usually boats moored on the far bank, this is where in the past there was the Oil Terminal where they pumped oil in and out of large container ships.

**(2)**

Then it is on through a few more bends and a walk past the Water Treatment Works on the right across the Exeter Ship Canal. Then it is on again to the final section which leads on up to the Exeter Ship Canal Swing Bridge.

**Exeter Ship Canal.**

# Chapter 7 Exeter Ship Canal Swing Bridge to Topsham

**Park & Start Grid ref; SX 966879**

**Distance: 2.5 Miles**

**Level: Easy**

**Time: 1 hour 45 minutes**

**Terrain: cycle track and pathway along the canal tow-path.**

**Maps.  O.S Explorer 110 Torquay and Dawlish.**

**Refreshments: None nearby a walk to Exminster or optional into Exeter.**

**The main road bridge over the River Exe into Countess Wear.**

**One of the new bridges over the River Clyst for pedestrians and cyclist.**

### Access to start

Leave M5 motorway at junction 30 and then exit the roundabout at 1st exit onto the Sidmouth Road. Then at next roundabout take 2nd exit onto the A376 still on the Sidmouth Road. Carry on through the next two roundabouts on the A376, then after about 2 miles take the 2nd exit off roundabout go past Darts Farm Complex and on towards Bridge Hill then on to Elmgrove Road into Topsham.

## Places Nearby

### Topsham

Topsham in the early days became the port of the Roman City of Isca Dumnoniorum (**Exeter**) in the first century AD and continued to serve it until the Roman Occupation of the South of Britain ceased about the year 400 AD. In the 7th century the Saxon rule in East Devon saw the settlement grow into a considerable village. Today it is a tranquil town set on the edge of the Exe Estuary with its many Dutch style houses from the time when Topsham was an important cotton port. Topsham Museum is located in a set of 17th century buildings looking out over the Exe Estuary. It consist of furnished period rooms, a display of the local history of the town and memorabilia of Vivien Leigh the film star.

### Bowling green Marshes

The marshes are a very impressive winter site for a large number of waders and wildfowl birds. This area is managed by the RSPB, and the birds can be viewed from hides along the boardwalk over the wetland which forms part of the Exe Estuary Trail into Exton.

**Overlooking the wetlands at Bowling Green Marshes**

**The Walk**

**(1)**

On exiting the canal tow-path at Exeter Ship Canal Swing Bridge turn right onto Exeter Road, which is then taking you back onto the main walk do not cross road and follow path over the old bridge over the River Exe and continue on to take the next turning right into Glasshouse Lane. (At this point if you are a cyclist then please cross the road at the pedestrian crossing and follow track on opposite side of road safely up to the next pedestrian crossing, then cross road to enter into Glasshouse Lane). Continue to follow Glasshouse Lane up a slope and down the other side to reach a sharp left hand bend, just follow bend around ignoring the public footpath sign to Topsham on the right. Stay on Glasshouse Lane around the bend for another 150 metres and then take the first right onto Wear Barton Road, continue on this road for about another 200 metres before taking the first turning left into Higher Wear Road. Then after about another 250 metres turn right onto Newport Road. Stay on Newport Road around the twist and turns to the end as it then veers out to meet the cycle track on Topsham Road.

**(2)**

Follow the cycle track on along Topsham Road for a short distance to a pedestrian crossing, cross over road to pick-up cycle/pedestrian track on the other side of the road. Follow track on in towards Topsham go under the M5 motorway where the road then changes into Exeter Road, then just past Topsham Town Football ground look out on the track for sign pointing down right to Ashford Road on the opposite side marked cycle route 2. **Option 3** At this point there is an alternative route and that is to turn left up Denver Road just after the football ground on the same side. Follow Denver Road up and around and under the railway bridge to reach junction of Clyst Road. Turn right at Clyst Road and follow to junction of Elmgrove Road keep to the left follow the road down past the Bridge Inn on left to cross road on cycle track over the new bridge across the River Clyst to follow on to Darts Farm for refreshments before re-joining the Exe Estuary Trail which is well marked from Darts Farm.

If however you do not want to go that way then stick to main route down Ashford Road on the other side of road. Follow the road for about 300 metres to the bottom of slope and turn left the only way to go onto Ferry Road, follow for almost a mile past the ferry terminal along the way from Exminster, on to the end at the junction of Fore Street. Then keep over to the right and follow road onto the Strand.

**New Cycle Bridge over River Clyst on the way to Darts Farm.**

# Chapter 8 Topsham to Exton

**Park & Start Grid ref; SX 978869**

**Distance: 2 Miles**

**Level: Easy**

**Time: 1 hour 30 minutes**

**Terrain: cycle track, quiet roads.**

**Maps.  O.S Explorer 110 Torquay and Dawlish.**

**Refreshments: Plenty of cafes, pubs and restaurants in Topsham.**

**New Bridge over River Clyst across wetland to link with Exton.**

Picture taken from the new Bridge looking across the River Clyst.

**Access to start**

Leave M5 motorway at junction 30 and then exit the roundabout at 1st exit onto the Sidmouth Road. Then at next roundabout take 2nd exit onto the A376 still on the Sidmouth Road. Carry on through the next two roundabouts on the A376, then after about 2 miles take the 2nd exit off roundabout go past Darts Farm Complex, do you're shopping have a coffee and cross the road and you are in Exton.

**Places Nearby**

**Option 3**

After coming along Topsham Road and turning up Denver Road described in text head for Darts Farm Complex, turn right at the pedestrian crossing down a narrow footpath at the back of Odhams Wharf, and follow the narrow path as it weaves its way through the quaint cottages turning right at the signpost to Lympstone. Follow past the warehouses at the edge of the docks to finally link up with the new Exe Estuary Trail from Topsham over the marshes connected by the new bridge over the River Clyst.

**Exton**

Just a small village with the views over the Exe Estuary and the Puffing Billy pub for coffee and lunch.

**The Walk**

**(1)**

So may be after a short stay in Topsham, continue on the walk along the Strand. Stay on the Strand all the way to the end to reach the water side, and at this point you pick-up the Goat Walk **(please note there is no cycling on this section)**. This is only a short distance to the end where you turn left onto Bowling Green Road, stay on this road for almost a mile to where the road starts to rise. Before starting to climb up slope turn right onto a marked Exe Estuary Trail to go under a railway bridge.

**(2)**

Now once you are under the railway bridge this then takes you onto the new boardwalk across Bowling Green Marsh for about half a mile, you then go on over the new bridge built across the River Clyst. After crossing the new bridge you reach a junction off to the left and turning down here will take you off to Darts Farm or on in a circle back to Topsham. But for the purpose of the Exe Estuary Trail walk continue straight on for about another mile to reach a left hand bend in the trail which will lead on into Exton.

**New Bridge over the River Clyst.**

# Chapter 9 Exton to Lympstone

Park & Start Grid ref; SX 989841

Distance: 2 Miles

Level: Easy

Time: 1 hour 30 minutes

Terrain: cycle track, quiet roads.

Maps.  O.S Explorer 110 Torquay and Dawlish.

Refreshments: Puffing Billy, Shears Café Lympstone.

Powderham Folly from the other side the Exe Estuary.

**Exe Estuary Trail on the way to Lympstone.**

## Access to start

Leave M5 motorway at junction 30 and then exit the roundabout at 1st exit onto the Sidmouth Road. Then at next roundabout take 2nd exit onto the A376 still on the Sidmouth Road. Carry on through the next two roundabouts on the A376, then after about 2 miles take the 1st exit off roundabout and carry straight on in the direction of Exmouth, then just past the Nutwell Lodge Hotel on left take the road on the right straight into Lympstone.

## Places Nearby

### Lympstone

This is a small village on the edge of the Exe Estuary, it is however known locally for Peter's Tower an Italianate riverfront brick clock built around 1885 by W.H. Peters as a memorial to his wife. Nearby to Lympstone is the Commando Training Centre for Royal Marines which as its own dedicated railway halt. In the 1990's the lead guitarist of the Kinks, Dave Davies lived in Lympstone.

**The Walk**

**(1)**

After going past the sharp left hand bend follow lane up to the left ignoring the private drive on right, continue on up to the main lane and turn right onto Green lane. Stay on Green Lane right the way through the village to finally reach a road junction at the end. Turn right at the road junction to walk past the Puffing Billy Pub on the right, this is a good place to stop for refreshments. Then carry on down the road towards the railway station, just before rail station and car park turn left onto the Exe Estuary Trail which is very clearly marked. Then stay on the Exe Estuary Trail for over a mile making sure you soak up the views out over the estuary to Dawlish Warren, go on past the Royal Marine Commando Training Centre, and further on you go past the Ornamental Lake and then on into Lympstone, up the slope and across the railway bridge then down the other side into the railway car park. Then follow the pedestrian path on the left down to The Strand the road at the bottom of the slope, at this point there is Shears Café straight across the road which is dog friendly.

**View of the Exe Estuary just before Lympstone.**

# Chapter 10 Lympstone to Exmouth

**Park & Start Grid ref; SX 998811**

**Distance: 2.5 Miles**

**Level: Easy**

**Time: 1 hour 30 minutes**

**Terrain: cycle track, quiet roads**

**Maps.  O.S Explorer 110 Torquay and Dawlish.**

**Refreshments: Puffing Billy pub Exton Shears Café Lympstone.**

**Tranquil area in Lympstone.**

**The view back towards Lympstone with the reeds on the right.**

## Access to start

Leave M5 motorway at junction 30 and then exit the roundabout at 1st exit onto the Sidmouth Road. Then at next roundabout take 2nd exit onto the A376 still on the Sidmouth Road. Carry on through the next two roundabouts on the A376, then after about 2 miles take the 1st exit off roundabout and carry straight on into Exmouth.

### Places Nearby

### Exmouth

Exmouth is positioned at the very start of the Jurassic Coast which is a U.N.E.S.C.O. World Heritage Site. So by walking the Southwest Coast Path it is an excellent way to explore the Jurassic Coast line. The whole Exmouth area is steeped in history with Byzantine coins dating back to 498-518 marked Anastasius 1 where found on the beach, and at Exmouth Point human occupation can be traced back to the 11th century.

### A la Ronde

This is an unusual 18th century house wonderful interior decoration and a collection of 25,000 shells nicely encrusted in the galley. The sixteen sided house was once described by Lucinda Lambton as having a magical strangeness that one might dream of as a child.

**The Walk**

**(1)**

Once in Lympstone the walk continues on past Shears Café and along the Strand which soon changes into Sowden Lane as it sweeps around a bend and then up hill. Stay on Sowden Lane for a half a mile passing Highcliffe House on the right, and then on past Highcliffe Close on the left. This then brings you to the top of the hill, then as you drop down the other side look at the magnificent views to the right down to Exmouth and across the Exe Estuary to Starcross and Dawlish Warren. Then at the bottom of the hill Sowden Lane then swings left around a very sharp bend, then after about 150 metres up on the right you go through a gateway to pick-up the off road Exe Estuary Trail.

**(2)**

The off road Exe Estuary Trail now continues on for about 1.5 miles great views off to the right out over the Exe Estuary. Then further on you go past Halsdon Farm which is now owned by the National Trust. Then at the end of the off road Exe Estuary Trail you exit via a gate and then continue along Mudbank Lane past Halsdon Avenue on the left, then on to cross a bridge on the right into Carter Avenue. After about 100 metres down the Avenue and just at the end of a left hand bend turn right through a gate into a park, and then follow pathway through the park past the football ground to the end. Then Exit Park through gate onto a pedestrian/cyclist shared path running parallel with the main road into Exmouth. Once at the end of the pathway the National Cycle Route 2 continues onto the seafront, but the Exe Estuary Trail is completed. At this point there is the bus station and rail station both at the end on the right hand side ready for the journey home.

**The Boardwalk across the wetter areas on the Exe Estuary Trail.**

# Special Travel Features.

**Bus Service**

**Route 2**

**Newton Abbot – Teignmouth – Dawlish - Cockwood Harbour – Starcross – Kenton – Exminster – Exeter.**

**Runs Monday to Saturday daytime every 20 minutes and Sunday every 30 minutes from the spring, services run hourly during evenings and winter.**

**Route 57**

**Exeter – Topsham – Exton – Lympstone – Exmouth.**

**Runs Monday to Saturday daytime every 15 minutes and Sunday and evenings every 30 minutes.**

**Trains**

**Check Trainline.com on website.**

**Topsham Ferry**

## Times of operation

These depend on tide and weather conditions, so please call 07801 203338 before travelling (also for evening water taxi service). Summer (April to September) Daily except Tuesdays 9.30am to 5.30pm (except at low tides)

Winter: Weekends and bank holidays

- 10.00am to 5.00pm (except at low tides)

## Fares

(From April 2014) subject to change in 2015

- One way fare £1.10 per person (under 5 years old free) Dogs, bicycles, pushchairs etc. 60p.

**Devon Cruises with Stuart Line.**

The easiest way to see the wonderful wildlife of the River Exe and the historic landscape of the Jurassic Coast.

Check on website www.stuartlinecruises.co.uk or phone 01395 222144

There are circular cruises on the River Exe, warm winter river cruise or guided bird watching trips.

Then you can sail the oldest shipping Exeter Canal through two working locks and the Countess Weir Swing Bridge, these are one way from Exmouth or from Exeter.

The Sea Dream II runs a boat between Topsham and the Turf Lock 07778 370582.

The White Heather runs from Double Locks to Turf Lock 07984 368442.

Exeter Cruises run a boat from Exeter Quay to the Double Locks 07984 368442.

**Water Taxi**

The water taxi runs from Exmouth to Dawlish Warren 07970 918418.

Please remember bookings may be necessary for some ferry services.

**Bike Hire**

**Saddles and Paddles** 01392 424241 www.saddlepaddle.co.uk

Hire canoes and bicycles and are located on the Exeter Quayside.

**Route2** Café and bicycle hire 01392 875085 located on Topsham quayside.

**Exmouth Cycles** 01395 225656 Bicycle shop and hire. Located on Victoria Road Exmouth.

**Knobblies Cycle Shop**

Bicycle shop and hire also located on Victoria Road Exmouth.

**Starcross to Exmouth Foot Ferry**

A typical crossing time is 15-20 minutes, depending on tides.

Starcross Pier is accessed by steps via the railway station bridge at Starcross Station. Please bear this in mind if you are using heavy bicycles, tandem/trailers and pushchairs.

This ferry service links up with National Route 2 of the National Cycle Network and cycles can be carried on the ferry for a small additional charge.

Ferries may be busy at peak times but we will do our best to carry as many cycles as space/regulations allow. We regret we are unable to pre book seats and cycle

# Ferries from Starcross

Park your car in the car park just up the road from the railway station. Cross the footbridge to our private pier.

## Timetable from Starcross subject to change in 2015 check website.

- 10.10am and 10 minutes past the hour until
- 5.10pm *

# Ferries from Exmouth

The ferry departs and arrives at Exmouth Marina, just a short walk to the beach or a 10 minute stroll in to the centre of town.

## Timetable from Exmouth may change in 2015.

- 10.40am 40 minutes to the hour until 5.40pm *

Meandering Walking Series other titles also published.

Meandering in Mid Devon

Meandering in South Devon

Meandering on Rivers and Canals in Devon

Meandering Pub Walks in Devon

Meandering Tea Room Walks in Devon

Meandering in Gloucestershire

Website

http://johncoombes.wix.com/meandering-walks-2

Photos of all the walks.

John coombes google plus

Printed in Great Britain
by Amazon

37273912R00027